Marisa Wohlschlaeger

ISSUE 7   October 2018

LOUD & QUEER

QUEER VOICES

OF NOW

QUEER HALLOWEEN

Marisa Wohlschlaeger

QUEER HALLOWEEN

For many of us, Halloween is a favorite time of year. The comfort of fall setting in and the freedom to dress in costumes brings joy every year. The mystery of magic and fright of the horrific is a part of what makes this time exciting. Every year a new chance to be someone new and find a new piece of yourself. Share your celebrations with us @loudandqueerzine !

Because this zine contains the exciting and the scary, the zine includes some content that isn't suitable for everyone. Please note the content warnings in the table of contents and at the top of each page.

Thank you for being a part of the LOUD & QUEER community. your interest and support is what allows us to create this zine and share queer voices of now.

BECOME A PATRON OF LOUD & QUEER ZINE AT **PATREON.COM/LOUDANDQUEERZINE**

CONTENTS

Content Warning Legend

[1] Violence   [2] Suicide   [3] Explicit Language

[4] Nudity   [5] Drugs

Stars Bursting Inside Me
By Maddie Silva

I.
Your mouth is full of stars,
When you speak, only dust comes out.
Yet when you touch me,
all I see are constellations.

II.
Draw me a universe, love.
With eyes that drip in joy,
placing laughter in the air,
beauty falls over you so well.
Veins like fault lines,
earthquakes cradled inside your lungs
trembling in concrete shoes.
I know that darkness is a friend that visits you often
and sleeps in your bed,
I know that love comes to you easy
but it is trust that never looks you in the eye.
I know you have been broken
and you're not sure where some pieces have gone.
My love,
you are creating land
carving pieces into stone
you are your own universe.

Landscapes are not made from the fine touch of a designer

but from the voracious finger-painter with dirt under her nails
and the unsteady artist looking for her style
Art is searching
So when you see something beautiful
It's because it's been journeying for a while

So please do not worry, I'm a mess too
We'll entangle each other in the disasters we've inherited
Two goddesses making art out of debris
Shaping universes of many stars and little moons
Draw me this universe, Love.

III.
shoplifting and dealing to friends and dumpster diving with the
headlights on
and sometimes with the gear in drive
and most times with the bummer in the back

finesse and lust and sex with a capital X
and sometimes with a question mark
and most times with a dot-dot-dot

hard marks and sweaty apologies and crying that sounds like
screaming
and sometimes like begging
and most times like out-of-reach truth
signs and cameras and statements that are with the movement
and sometimes against the movement
and most times of the movement

crushed chests and behind-doors violence and tears during sex as-
sault
and sometimes during protests
and most times during breakfast in the parked car
pooling beer and bubblers and lines on lines that taste like yester-
day
and sometimes like kisses
and most times like family holidays

noise and skin and celebrations that come from streets under
streets
and sometimes from digging nails into knees
and most times from the poison air we can't see
exes and periods that keep coming and songs we can't listen to
and sometimes can't remember
and most times sing to ourselves

wedding dresses and kids in cribs and heaven that filters through
cobwebs
and sometimes through our decade-old eyes
and most times through shadows and doubles holding hands

Note from the writer:

Based in Los Angeles, Maddie currently works at the Natural History Museum and enjoys writing, drawing, and going on adventures. Her most recent adventure is attempting to make her own zines!

Find her drawing here: @int._artroom_day

Sarah
By Sean White

Some days I still grieve

My given name , the one I can't bare to speak

each gender performance that screamed out "liar" in the mirror

The softness of performing what they call femininity

Sometimes I have to allow myself to think about my roots

That I have the power to grow life inside me

My body syncs with the moon when I allow it to .

Even through the beauty I just can't allow myself to bleed without wanting to everywhere

Everywhere I go , I feel the mask that most don't know is there

My body speaks almost nothing of what it's actually seen

Prison of performance that sometimes feels like I'm hiding in plain sight

Everyone else is always locking me up into new chains of what I should be

Living out of the suitcase of masculinity

I can't even begin to unpack

But the truth is , my soul has never been more at home

Sometimes you just have to forgive yourself for the person you could never be so you can call yourself a home.

Note from the writer:

My name is Sean White, I'm a 22 year old poet, barista, and an aspiring filmmaker from Austin , TX. I am transmasculine and I use they/them pronouns. My piece called "Sarah" is basically a love letter for my birth name and the feeling you get saying goodbye to a part of yourself, even if it's not serving you anymore. This comes from a very personal place.

Untitled et al
By Michael Tatarnikov

Note from the artist:

My name is Mikhail Tatarnikov an Artist a citizen of the Netherlands , living in Maastricht city. I want to be useful to the community , I am a self-taught artist. I am just a beginner, but I would like to become a member of every art community

CABIN IN THE WOODS
REMOTE YOOPER MICHIGAN
HERE IT IS!
BY JASON A. QUEST

A JAQRABBIT TALE - OCTOBER 2009
HASN'T CHANGED SINCE JAY AND I WERE HERE, BACK IN ... 2002?

BUT JUST ME AND THE RIVER NOW.
© TALES.JAQRABBIT.COM

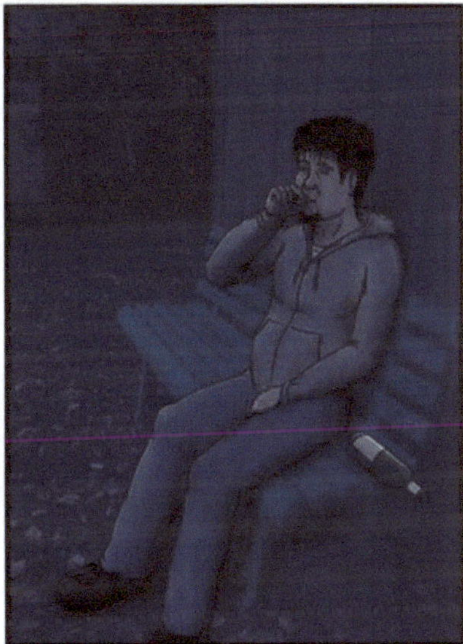

SNAP!

WHO'S THERE?
HI! IT'S ME!

IT CAN'T BE!
YOU DIED, JAY!
YOU KNOW I DON'T BELIEVE IN GHOSTS!

BUT LOOK AT THE EVIDENCE!

HERE I AM!
BUT...

I MISS YOU!
© TALES.JAQRABBIT.COM

THAT'S WHY I'M HERE.

© TALES.JAQRABBIT.COM

© TALES.JAQRABBIT.COM

HOW'S YOUR LOVE LIFE OTHERWISE?
OK, I GUESS.

ANYONE SPECIAL?
NOT SINCE YOU.

YOU SILLY ASS!

YOU'RE SUPPOSED TO GO ON WITH YOUR LIFE!

I WANTED YOU TO BE HAPPY!

Note from the creator:

I'm a middle-aged queer cartoonist from West Michigan. My work has been featured in "Best Gay Erotica 2014" and "RFD" magazine, and I am currently serializing my quasi-bio-pornographic novel "JAQrabbit Tales".

Love is a Danger

By Drew Payne

"A threesome? How do I know your boyfriend's not some old dog," he said.

So I showed him the picture, on my phone, of Jonathan and me taken when we were on holiday.

"He's hot," the guy said.

"Let's go then," I said.

I led him out of the club.

"I haven't the cash for a taxi," he said.

"Don't worry, my car is parked around the corner," I said.

On the drive to my house he chatted away about himself, it was his only topic of conversation, but he'd been easy to pick-up. I'm reasonably attractive, Nana taught me a few things to hold someone's attention, and the vain ones are the easiest to get. Jonathan needed his company.

I inherited my house when my parents died in a car crash. No one my age could normally afford a three floored, detached house in Forrest Gate, London.

The house was dark when we reached it, but that was normal. I took him inside (I make sure never to remember their names now) and took him to the basement.

"Where we going?" he asked.

"It's our little playroom," I said

"Cool."

I opened the door to the basement's room, were Jonathan was waiting.

"After you," I said.

Smiling he walked in and I followed.

Jonathan was sat in the centre of the room. He was only wearing an old pair of jogging bottoms. His skin was grey, his hair was flat and dull, his body was slumped down and weak, there was no life in his eyes. He looked on the verge of death.

"You liar! He looks like shit!" The guy said.

"Please…" Jonathan said as he stood up.

"I'm out of here," the guy said.

"He needs you," I said and pushed him back into Jonathan's arms.

"Thank you," Jonathan said, and then bit into the guy's neck, ripping off the flesh.

I closed the door on them. I climbed up to our bedroom on the first floor; up there I wouldn't hear any noise or screams from the basement.

In our bedroom I had a shower and then got into bed, naked.

***

Jonathan was the love of my life but our relationship was so short. He was troubled and deeply in the closet, he'd rarely go anywhere with me. His father was a notorious Evangelical Anglican Minister, so I shouldn't have expected more.

I was me who had found Jonathan though, that day.

The night before, his father had stormed into Jonathan's flat and found us together. He threw me out of there, as he screamed at Jonathan.

I kept calling Jonathan the all next day but nothing, the calls always went to voicemail. In the end I was so desperate I went back to his flat. I found him still in bed but he was dead. He'd taken an overdose.

I went crazy with grief. I wrapped Jonathan in his duvet, took him down to my car and drove him to my home. There I laid him out in one of the bedrooms. Then I sat by his body and wept.

I eventually moved the next day. I went to the only person I knew who could help me, my Nana.

My maternal grandmother, my Nana, is Creole. She came to Britain during the Second World War where she met and married my grandfather. Though he died years ago, she still lives in her home in Peckham. Most people think of her as one of Peckham's little old ladies, they don't know she's a Santerian Priestess. Santerian is an ancient religion and Nana has practiced it all her life, but she doesn't tell many others because people can be very closed minded.

"What's the matter my love?" She said as she opened the door to me.

Through my sobs I told her what had happened and when I'd finished she simply said:

"Do you want him back?"

"Nana, yes."

"Then take me to your man."

I drove her back to my house, with her "ceremonial" bag; then I took her up to the room were Jonathan was. She told me to wait outside while she went into the bedroom alone.

I sat outside and waited. I heard Nana praying and chanting for an age in there. I just waited.

Then her chanting stopped and moments later I heard someone else coughing. Nana opened the door and behind her I saw Jonathan, sitting up on the bed, alive again. I ran past her and through my arms around him.

"Where've you been?" Jonathan asked me.

Much later, as I was driving her home, Nana warned me:

"I bought your man back from the world of the dead. He's not dead or alive so he has no life-energy of his own. You have to find him that energy, each month."

"Where do I find it?" I asked.

"Living flesh. He has to eat the living flesh of a human. They can't be dead, they must be living when he eats them. Can you do that? If you can't you'll lose him forever."

"I can do it," I said.

***

The first time I bought someone back for Jonathan was the hardest. I made the mistake of remembering his name and listening to him. I felt sick when I handed him over to Jonathan, but it was worth it to have Jonathan back.

After that it was easier because I didn't think of them as real, just food for Jonathan, I thought only of Jonathan.

***

I must have dosed off because I was waken up by Jonathan coming into our bedroom. He was naked but his hair was once more blonde, his skin glowed, his eyes were alive again, he was beautiful again.

"I'll clean the cellar up later," he said as he got into bed with me.

"I love you," I said, as I kissed him deeply.

We fell back onto the bed and started to make love, again.

Saying Goodbye to Mickey

By Drew Payne

"Right, I'll get our after dinner entertainment," Liam announced, jumping up and the table and dashing out of the room.

"God, what's he got planned," Chris said.

Dan shot him "a look" but Chris ignored him. This evening been planned for George and he didn't want Chris going off in one of his bitching moods, his lover had been in entertaining form so far. The four of them (Dan, his lover Chris, George and their host Liam) had enjoyed a meal together in Liam's comfortable home. Liam was certainly a good host.

The evening had been Liam's idea; he'd said they needed to do it for George and Dan and Chris had readily agreed. Dan had been so concerned about George these last few weeks. It was barely four weeks ago that Mickey, George's lover, had died.

Mickey had cancer, which was slowly eaten away at him. He'd lived through five years of different treatments but all they did was make him weaker and weaker. When he died he'd looked like a wasted, little old man, far older than his forty-five years.

Dan had also watched Mickey's illness take its toll on George. He'd seemed helpless in the face of Mickey's slow decline, yet George had borne it all silently. He'd never discussed with any of them how he was feeling, keeping his feelings tight to himself. Even when Mickey died George had kept himself quiet, barely shedding a tear at Mickey's funeral, and they'd been lovers for nearly twenty years.

It was the way Mickey died that had so disturbed Dan. Mickey had been sleeping on the sofa, he'd been having a restless night, but when George woke the next morning he'd found Mickey dead, still lying on the sofa. Dan felt a shudder run through him when he heard this, if he'd lost Chris like that he didn't think he could have coped. George, though, had said nothing about it. He had seemed to wrap his grief away inside of himself.

Liam came back into the room, carrying a large, elaborate wooden board; which he set down in the middle of the dining table.

"Here it is!" He said, with a flourish.

Dan felt his stomach sink when he saw what it was.

"It's a Ouija Board," Chris said.

"Yes," Liam said, as he sat down. "I thought we could have ago with it."

"I don't think so," George said.

"Come on this will be interesting," Liam said.

"Why?" Chris asked.

But Dan realised what Liam was up to and his stomach tied itself into a tight knot.

"So George can speak to Mickey," Liam said.

"No, really, no," George said.

"Come on, just give it ago," Liam said.

"I don't know," George said.

"It's harmless," Liam said.

"Yeah, we used to do it when we were kids," Chris said. "Nothing really happened."

"Are you sure," George said.

"Yeah, nothing ever happened," Chris said.

"Okay, but no messing about and faking you're the devil or someone else," George said.

"No one would do that," Liam said as he glanced at Chris and Dan.

"Okay, then," George said

"Right, the let's go ahead," Liam said.

Liam placed an upturn wineglass in the centre of the Ouija Board and the four of them placed their fingers on top if it. Doing so made Dan feel uncomfortable but he kept his finger there.

The four of them sat there, like that, for an awkward moment before Liam spoke:

"Is anyone here?"

In response there came silence.

"This is stupid," George said.

"Give it chance," Liam said. "Answer us, if you can hear us," Liam said again to the wineglass.

This time the glass gave a shudder and slid across the Ouija Board to the "Yes" symbol. Dan glanced over at Chris but he was staring intently at the wineglass.

"Who is it?" Liam asked.

The glass slid across the bored until it stopped over to the M, then it slid around to the I. In a handful of seconds it spelt out "Mickey".

"This is a joke," George hissed.

"No it isn't," Liam said.

Dan glanced at Chris but he was still staring at the glass.

"Is there's someone you want to talk to?" Liam asked the glass.

The glass quickly spelt out "George". Dan could feel the glass moving under his finger, but it felt as if the glass was moving by itself not as if anyone was pushing it.

"Do you want George to say goodbye to you?" Liam asked it.

The glass shot across to the "No".

"What you want to say?" Liam asked.

The glass now rushed round the Ouija Board, it quickly spelt out "why... did... you..." but it didn't finish. George jumped up from the table, knocking the glass over, and shouted:

"This is crap!"

Then the room's lights went out.

Dan jumped up from the table as he heard Chris shout:

"What's happening?"

The next moment the room's lights came back on. Dan looked about himself. Chris was still sat at the table, though the Ouija Board was pushed the end of it, but Liam was now stood over George and staring down at him. How had Liam moved so quickly?

The expression on Liam's face, one that Dan had never seen before, was of pure anger. Liam's expression reminded him of something.

"Liam, what's going on?" Dan said.

"Liam? Is that little whore here?" Liam snapped, his voice deep and rough with a completely different accent, a voice that sounded like Mickey's.

"Who are you?" Dan asked.

"Don't you recognise your old mate?" that voice came from Liam's mouth. Mickey's voice.

It was Mickey's expression twisting up the features of Liam's face.

"It's me, Mickey," he snarled.

Dan felt light-headed, this couldn't be true, Liam couldn't be possessed by Mickey's spirit?

"You're dead," George said.

"Don't you know it!" Liam/Mickey turned on him. "You only smoothed me with a fucking pillow!"

"You had cancer, you were in pain, I couldn't cope!" George shouted back.

"I could have lived for months but you killed me. You suffocated me in my sleep because you're so fucking weak!"

Liam/Mickey jumped forward and snatched hold of George's head. Just as quickly he began to repeatedly smacked George's head against the table. Dan was so shocked he just stood there.

"Stop them!" Chris shouted, snapping Dan out of his disbelief.

He rushed forward and grabbed hold of Liam/Mickey, pulling him off George. He struggled for a moment then he stopped, standing passively within Dan's arms.

Chris had taken hold of George and was lifting up his now lifeless body but it was too late. George's eyes were open but un-moving.

"He's dead," Chris said.

"Who's dead?" Liam said, in his normal voice.

"Oh God, who's going to believe this," Dan replied as he let go of Liam.

Note from the writer:

I live in London, England, and have been writing all my life. My writing has been published in a wide verity of magazines, journals and websites, both my fiction and non-fiction. My writing has been regularly performed as part of the Newsrevue show, the longest running satirical stage show in London. Some of my short stories can be found at:

https://tablo.io/drew-payne , my blog can be read at: https://drewpayne.blogspot.com/

QUEER IT
By Angelica Angeles

A very #QUEER version of the horror films "IT" and "Spawn"...

Everyone is afraid of something, A Clown.

Favorite Sweet Treat!

Creature that feeds and thrives on its vic-tim's FEAR.

PUFF! PUFF! Traps are way more effec-
tive when they are attractive.

Proceeded to lure them
with the promise of desserts
in the sewers.

PREDATOR!
ALONE, WEAK, VULNERABLE
(Clown ATTACKS)

Your fear makes the enemy stronger. The dancing clown! Creature that feeds and thrives on it's victim FEAR!

Everyone is afraid of something, A clown.

I'm weird...and I enjoy IT!

IF YOU ARE SCREAMING AND GAGGING FOR

"QUEER IT"

WE ARE RELEASING OUR QUEER IT ZINE ISSUE! COMING SOON! ;)

MEET THE CREATOR & MODEL

ANGELICA ANGELES

MEET MODEL

MARISA WOHLSCHLAEGER

FOLLOW US:
ANGELICA ANGELES
(ARIES_I_AM &
ARIESIAMPRODUCTION)
MARISA WOHLSCHLAEGER
(MARISATHERAINBOW &
LOUDANDQUEERZINE)
JAKE ROSE (LOOKATJAKEROSE)

PHOTOGRAPHER :
JAKE ROSE

BECOME A PART OF OUR QUEER COMMUNITY

Our community of creators always needs new voices to add to the zine. Want to become a part of LOUD & QUEER?

Submit your writing, art, or other creations to:

loudandqueerzine@gmail.com

Please include 1) your name, 2) the name of your piece(s), and 3) 1-2 sentences to share with our readers.

We will consider your work for our next issue!

Share our call for submissions with LGBTQIA+ creators everywhere so we can give them a voice too!

THANK YOU to all the artists, writers, and creators who submitted their work and featured their pieces in LOUD & QUEER. The zine wouldn't be possible without you!

SUPPORT
LOUD & QUEER
NOW & FOREVER

LOUD & QUEER is committed to giving a voice to the queer community and projecting those perspectives into the wider community. We want everyone to hear queer voices of now, and that is why our zine is given out freely to all that want to read it.

We rely on patrons and donations to keep the zine going. Did you love this issue? Want new issues of LOUD & QUEER in the future? Want to receive exclusive perks and rewards while supporting LGBTQIA+ creators?

Become a patron of LOUD & QUEER
PATREON.COM/LOUDANDQUEERZINE

* 9 7 9 8 3 5 3 2 3 4 5 5 5 *